THE
NENE VALLEY
RAILWAY

· A PAST and PRESENT COMPANION ·

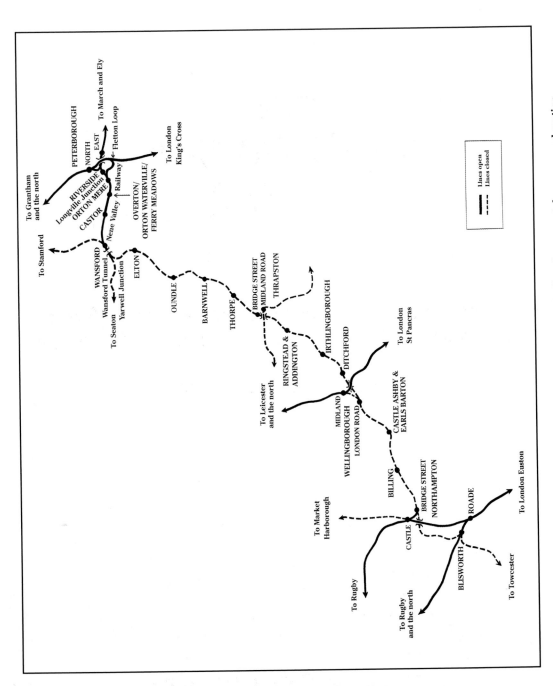

Map of the Nene Valley line and associated connections, including the present-day preserved section.

THE
NENE VALLEY RAILWAY

·A PAST and PRESENT COMPANION·

A nostalgic trip along the whole route from Blisworth and Northampton to Peterborough

Christopher Awdry

·RAILWAY HERITAGE·
from
The NOSTALGIA Collection

First published in 2001

British Library Cataloguing in Publication Data

A catalogue record for this book is available from the British Library.

ISBN 1 85895 170 4

Past & Present Publishing Ltd
The Trundle
Ringstead Road
Great Addington
Kettering
Northants NN14 4BW

Tel/Fax: 01536 330588
email: sales@nostalgiacollection.com

Main map drawn by Christina Siviter

Printed and bound in Great Britain

Past and Present

A Past & Present book
from
The NOSTALGIA *Collection*

ACKNOWLEDGEMENTS

I have been extremely grateful to many people during the preparation of this book, not least to Peter Townsend of Past & Present Publishing for suggesting it to me in the first place. Ken Fairey made his enormous collection of photographs available, while Peter Waszak did a similar service with the Nene Valley Railway's archive – to both I am greatly indebted, as I am also to many of Peter's colleagues at the NVR who helped to smooth the way. Of these I should mention in particular Mike Warrington, the NVR Manager, and emphasise that all pictures taken by me in what appear to be 'trespass' situations were taken with his knowledge and permission. To all other photographers who came to my assistance, my thanks also – all are acknowledged in the appropriate places.

I am grateful also for help in various forms to Fredon Engineering (Wellingborough); R. Jarvis (Whitworth Bros Ltd, Wellingborough); Tony Hayward (Oundle); Mrs Marion Grantham (Oundle); Mr Keith Goldsmith (Thorpe); Mrs Joy Holmes (Thrapston); and J. A. Hutchinson & Sons (Haulage) Ltd (Wansford).

Two small books that I found invaluable, and which I can recommend wholeheartedly to any reader who wishes to expand on what is found here, are *Peterborough's First Railway* by Peter Waszak and John W. Ginns, and *The Nene Valley Railway* by John Rhodes. Both are available from the NVR shop at Wansford.

Finally, though by no means least, I should acknowledge my wife Diana, who, apart from more material and recent assistance, unwittingly helped also when she suggested some 11 years ago that we move to Oundle – it is a move that neither of us has regretted.

CONTENTS

Wansford is the headquarters of the preserved Nene Valley Railway, and this familiar picture, the subject of an NVR postcard, shows a view not often visible these days, eastward along the platforms as they were in about 1912. Note the staggered platforms, linked by a lattice footbridge (no other station with staggered platforms along the line had one, which perhaps reflects the importance that was attached to Wansford). The nearest village, incidentally, is Sibson, and this was early recognised by its addition to the nameboard in brackets. The goods yard, with its shed at right-angles to the running line, stood on the north side.

The view is not often reproducible these days owing to the fact that carriage stock is usually stored in the left-hand platform road. A management tip-off, however, enabled me to be at the station on 12 September 1999, one of the few occasions when the train working left the platform empty for a few minutes, and I was thus able to reproduce the postcard picture. The platforms are now higher, are no longer staggered and the footbridge has been replaced, though it is in almost the same position as the original. The timber station building on Platform 1 is that rescued from Barnwell (see page 58), and was moved here by low-loader in 1977. *NVR Archives/CA*

INTRODUCTION

By the early 1840s the London & Birmingham Railway, having opened between those two cities in 1838, was beginning to have expansionist ideas. It was suggested by a delegation to the company from Northampton during the autumn of 1842 that a branch along the Nene Valley to Peterborough might be a sound idea; perhaps the company saw it as a way of appeasing some of the criticism it had received from those who thought its line should have gone through Northampton in the first place.

In any event, a survey was so quickly done that on 16 January 1843 a firm proposal was made to the proprietors. The company thought the line could be built economically, as indeed it was, and though not considered to be greatly profitable in itself, it would, the company felt, give useful access to East Anglia and Lincolnshire. In that area, it was expected, wide distribution of goods could be made by way of the various waterways.

There was opposition from some local landowners in the east, for since 1836 powers had been in place for a Northern & Eastern Railway to build a line from London to York. By 1843 this project had reached only Newport in Essex before running out of money, but the landowners must have had considerable faith in the scheme – and perhaps a large financial stake too – and one can understand their disquiet. In the end the Northern & Eastern got no further on its own, and the line to York eventually went through Peterborough. The Eastern Counties Railway was also aiming for Peterborough, with a branch from its line at Ely.

But the Nene Valley line – usually referred to as the Peterborough branch at first, though the other term quickly came into use – met few obstacles. After two meetings in March 1843 the Peterborough Cathedral Chapter agreed that the railway could use the Fair Meadow, part of its land on the south side of the river, in order to build its station, though in fact it never did so. By the time the line reached that point the Eastern Counties Railway had also obtained powers to build a station, and there was clearly no sense in making two so close together. So a rail link was agreed and a joint station proposed. In fact the joint arrangement fell through, and the London & Birmingham ended up being allowed to use the ECR's station.

After passing its Third Reading in the House of Commons by 31 votes on 9 May 1843, the Act scraped only narrowly (52/51) through its Second Reading in the Lords on 1 June, being passed by a House of Lords Committee three weeks later. On 26 June it passed its Third Reading in the Lords, and gained Royal Assent on 4 July, which, compared with some Railway Bills, was a very swift passage indeed! Estimates for the line totalled £500,000, and it actually cost £429,409 to build – this was economical, at under £10,000 a mile. For those who like to know equivalent present-day values for such things – and this is, after all, a 'Past & Present book' – £1,000 in 1845 would have had a value of £55,300 in 1995. The railway was completed within two years of its Parliamentary authorisation.

Robert Stephenson was instructed to lay out the line, and various construction contracts were allotted on 11 January 1844. The Engineer appointed was George Parker Bidder; a Devonian, he had been invited by Robert Stephenson to work on the London & Birmingham Railway in 1834. He became an assistant to George Stephenson in his Parliamentary work, and quickly built a reputation. He worked much with Robert Stephenson, both in Britain and abroad, and was, at 38 (just three years younger than Stephenson), perhaps a natural choice for the Nene Valley line.

The River Nene would require bridging 13 times, but apart from this the only engineering item of any substance was a 616-yard-long tunnel at Wansford. The 300 and upwards navvies who built this tunnel drew adverse comment from a local newspaper, and extra police were

The Nene Valley line had to cross the river 13 times. Looking west on an evening in September 1963, an unidentified 2-6-4T hurries away from Ringstead & Addington station with a stopping train for Peterborough. The river bridge is characteristic of a type used throughout the line.

By 26 May 1999 the overgrowth has encroached, but the bridge is still there, likewise, of course, the river. *Ian L. Wright/CA*

employed to keep order. Perhaps worse was that when the job was finished and the men went on their way, they left many unpaid bills at shops and with landladies, and '…have taken many women from the neighbourhood, and in some instances the wives of decent men and the mothers of families, who have been induced to rob their husbands and abscond.' (Letter in the *Stamford Mercury*, 28 March 1845)

The first engine was placed on the rails at Thrapston on 19 February 1845, having been previously drawn through Northampton by 16 horses. Directors of the company travelled over the line by special train on 3 May, and on the 31st an official opening train, complete with company and civic dignitaries, covered the 47½-mile route in 2½ hours, including stops at Northampton, Thrapston and Oundle. Many of the stations were still incomplete at this stage, but in spite of this the railway opened to the public two days later, on 2 June 1845.

A regular service began of three trains a day in each direction. The journey time to Northampton from Peterborough was 2 hours, and to London 4½ hours. From the start the line was equipped with electric telegraph, a service also made available to the public, which meant that London could be contacted in seconds – much the same sort of sensation for the folks of 1845, one imagines, as the sending of an e-mail to Australia or New Zealand is for us today.

The line was double from Blisworth to Northampton from the start, but the rest was built single at first with a crossing place at Thrapston. Doubling was soon begun beyond Northampton – the precaution of buying land for double track had already been taken – and on 15 December 1845 the first goods train ran. Several attractive Tudor-style station houses were designed by John Livock, not a name with which many will be familiar. He was born in 1814 and trained in Leicester as an architect. By 1837 he was already designing stations, and his first contract railway work seems to have been on the Nene Valley line, where he designed several fine buildings. Oundle station, and a similar one at Wansford, both now in private ownership, are the most notable that survive, though there are also good examples at Tamworth and Atherstone in Staffordshire. His last railway work was in 1854, though he continued in practice as an architect at least until 1877.

By August, when the company gained a contract for mail from the Post Office, the service had been almost doubled to five trains each way daily, but 1st and 2nd class accommodation was available only between London and Northampton; on the branch it was 3rd class or nothing. There were two trains a day on Sundays. Connections were made by road-coach (shades of today's bus-link) to Stamford from Wansford, and between Peterborough and Wisbech; a 7.45am departure from Wisbech (alternate mornings only, which are not specified!) linked with the 11.00am train to Northampton, and a coach drove to Wisbech (apparently every day) with passengers off the 3.00pm or earlier arrivals, reaching the fenland town at 6.30pm.

This level of service remained steady until 1879, when the opening of the link between Seaton and Yarwell Junction brought additional trains. By the First World War about 28 trains were stopping at Wansford daily, and by 1938 this had increased to 38. By 1950, however, the service along the Northampton line was down to four trains each day to Peterborough and six in the opposite direction, with extras on Saturdays. There were no trains along the Nene Valley line on Sundays. There were, of course, also freight services.

From Blisworth the line curved sharply eastward to cross the Grand Junction Canal and follow the course of its Northampton branch towards the county town, where the railway ran into a station on the west side of Bridge Street, the main road towards London. After crossing the road, the railway met for the first time the river it would follow, more or less, for the rest of its journey.

Northampton lies 120 feet lower than Blisworth – the main reason why both railway and canal at first avoided the place – so the line had fallen considerably by now. The station was on the southern side of the town, and now the line headed south-east to a crossing at Hardwater and a small station at Billing. Ironstone siding connections were made at Cogenhoe (Cucknow) and Whiston, but Castle Ashby & Earls Barton served two important villages placed one on either side of the valley – river and railway ran between them, the railway to the south of the river.

Wellingborough (later to gain the suffix 'London Road') also had its station on the south side of the town – until 1857 it was its only station. Ditchford lay beyond, then Irthlingborough, whose village stood on the north side of the river and whose station stood on the south. This was then unspoiled countryside, and is still pleasant enough, though the gravel extracting industry is everywhere apparent these days. Ringstead & Addington was a good mile from either of its villages, in the depths of the countryside, and soon after this the line curved northwards and ran into Thrapston.

Again two railways served the town, and again it was the L&B (which became the London & North Western Railway in 1846) who got there first, this time retaining a monopoly until 1866. Beyond Thrapston station the line meandered through fields close to the river until it reached Thorpe, where it curved away and began to climb over the neck of a spur, past Wigsthorpe, which had no station. Curving north again, and downhill, the railway reached Barnwell, and crossed the river twice before arriving at Oundle.

Oundle's station lay to the east of the town, separated from it by the river and a picturesque stone bridge. Beyond, Fotheringhay was passed, famous as the birthplace of Richard III and deathplace of Mary Queen of Scots, but not considered worthy of a station on either account. Then came Elton, a small stopping place an easy mile and a half from its village, with Nassington as far in the opposite direction. Elton was an early casualty. Beyond Elton the line curved eastward to traverse Wansford tunnel, and soon after emerging ran into Wansford station.

From Yarwell Junction, just to the west of the tunnel, the railway is still alive, thanks to the Nene Valley Railway, a heritage line that began operations here in 1977. Another river crossing beyond the station leads close to the old Roman site of Durobrivae, and also the site where, near Castor station, the Romans' Ermine Street had crossed the river. Castor, again some distance from its village, lay to the north of the line and, set on its south-facing hillside, can be clearly seen from it. Overton station, another early casualty, has now become the Nene Valley Railway's Ferry Meadows station, and thereafter the line hugs the southern riverbank closely, through a new station, Orton Mere, into Peterborough. The NVR station is sited close to where the old LNWR engine shed once stood – the original line ran on, beneath the viaduct, to Peterborough East station, which lay just to the east of the present road viaduct across river and railway, and just north of Peterborough United's London Road football ground.

The Nene Valley line was one that served its local people well, but in the end there were insufficient of them using it to justify its working. The Modernisation Plan of 1959 suggested it as a possible closure, and Dr Beeching's Report in 1962 said the same. So it went. The section between Oundle and Peterborough survived, for various reasons, for longer, and thus, in part, has survived to form the present-day Nene Valley Railway. The steam facilities here continue to give enjoyment to many – long may it remain so.

Blisworth and Northampton Castle

The choice of site for a station at Blisworth was the purely arbitrary one of its being convenient for the start of a branch to Northampton. It lay about a mile north-west of the village for which it was named, and ultimately became the junction also for a highly impecunious branch line to Towcester and points west. Tracks for this branch can be seen to the right of the train in our first picture, beyond the signal box that looks, to judge from the removal of the steps, as if it has been closed. Passenger services on the branch had ceased ten years before this picture, though the goods traffic was to survive for two more years. Hastening north with a down Perth express on 12 June 1962 is Stanier 'Princess Coronation' 'Pacific' No 46250 *City of Lichfield*.

From the same place on 24 August 1999 the site of the signal box is obscured by vegetation as an unidentified Class 87 electric locomotive also heads north with the 09.35 ex-Euston Virgin Trains service to Preston. Blisworth station, now completely obliterated, lay where the rear of the train is, and the course of the branch to Northampton can be seen leading left opposite the rear three carriages. *Ken Fairey/CA*

An LNWR branch line opened on 16 February 1859 (part of which is now the site of the preserved Northampton & Lamport Railway) running north from Northampton station (later Bridge Street) to Market Harborough, via a small station near Northampton's castle. This Castle station was rebuilt when the loop from the main line at Roade reached the town in 1882, though the section north to Rugby had been opened the previous year; the castle was demolished in 1880 to make way for the new goods shed. On 2 May 1964 'Jubilee' Class 4-6-0 No 45672 *Anson* heads a goods train southwards into the station on the up through road past Northampton No 1 signal box, a standard LNWR Type 4 Size N box. This picture shows a wonderful display of semaphore signalling now, alas, no more. In 1959 No 45672 had been a Carlisle Upperby engine.

In the view north from Northampton's down platform on 13 August 1999 the main point of reference is the bridge in the distance. The colour light signal seems to be in more or less the same position as the right-hand support of the semaphore gantry in the 1964 picture. Note also that the platform has been built forward across the area previously used by the platform road; the old down through line is now the down platform line, and the single through track (the old up one) has become bi-directional. The up platform has been considerably extended, too. The approaching electric multiple unit (EMU), No 321414, is empty coaching stock to form the 11.30 departure for Milton Keynes and Euston only. *Ken Fairey/CA*

13

Turning round to look into the station, we see Fowler '4MT' 2-6-2T No 42331 waiting to depart with a train for Market Harborough on 31 December 1959, the final week of passenger services – the official closure date was 4 January 1960, though freight services lasted another four years. I remember Castle station (in the early 1950s) as rather dark – clearly my visits at that time never took me to this end of the platform!

Castle station – renamed plain Northampton after Bridge Street station closed – has changed greatly since 1959. Though the down platform and its building are in more or less the same place, the only real point of reference between these two pictures is the distant road bridge, glimpsed on the right of the pictures. As two railway employees head back to work, the driver of EMU set No 321427 prepares to leave with the 11.19 for Birmingham New Street on 13 August 1999. *Ken Fairey/CA*

We are now further into the station on a dismal day (5 January) in 1957, which rather bears out my gloomy remembrances of the place, although you must bear in mind that I would have been on my way to school at the time...! Facing north on the through road on this occasion is Class '4P' 4-4-0 No 40937 – this was a Deeley development of a Johnson Midland Railway three-cylinder compound introduced in 1905. It was later superheated by Fowler.

It has to be said that the station looks pleasanter now, however much one may regret the passing of the old order – an empty through road on this occasion allows us to see the new up-side buildings. There is a new footbridge too, though sited in the same place as previously, and the bay platforms from which the Peterborough service ran were on the left beyond it and the road overbridge. The EMU stock that has just drawn into the platform on the extreme right on 13 August 1999 is a terminating Silverlink train from Euston. *H. C. Casserley/CA*

These are the south-facing bay platforms at Castle from which the trains heading along the Nene Valley left, seen on the last day of the 'Wellingborough Motor', 2 May 1964. The honour of being in charge had been given to Kettering (15B) 2-6-2T No 41225, and the fireman is making sure the water supply lasts out. These Ivatt-designed taper-boilered engines were introduced in 1946, working at a boiler-pressure of 200psi – by 1964 No 41225 can barely be said to have worked her allotted span, but examples of the class are preserved on the Lakeside & Haverthwaite Railway in Cumbria.

Well, the bridge is still there, and a bit of platform coping forms an area of ground surface on the right, but there isn't a lot else that is recognisable. The new main entrance to the station can just be seen through the portal of the bridge, but on 13 August 1999 evidence of an erstwhile railway is meagre. *Ken Fairey/CA*

Trains to Bedford also used the south-facing bays at Northampton Castle, and on 24 September 1955 2-6-2T No 41270 is at the head of just such a service. When Northampton St John's, the Midland Railway station, closed to passengers on 3 July 1939, the connection with the LNWR lines was reversed and trains were diverted to Castle. So this train would, as it were, turn right just east of Northampton Bridge Street and reach its destination by way of a branch through Olney, joining the Midland main line south of Oakley. The passenger service ceased on 5 March 1962, and the line closed completely on 6 January 1964.

On 13 August 1999 one can deduce that the line of buried stones in the centre records the edge of the former platform, but there is little else that marks the area. To the left, through the bridge, is a view along the down platform of the main station. *H. C. Casserley/CA*

Looking outwards from the Northampton Castle bay platforms on 2 May 1964, 2-6-2T No 41225 leaves with the 'Wellingborough Motor' on the final day of its service. The 'Motor' made ten trips daily in 1960, and there was probably little variation to the end. The shadows seem to indicate an afternoon departure, so that while this may not be the very last train, time is clearly running out.

By 13 August 1999 the graffiti artists have had plenty of time to get busy, notwithstanding that this area is fenced off from the car-park – and perhaps it should be emphasised that this picture was taken from the right side of the fence! Change and decay are evident, though the girders of the bridge – spanning a stream – appear unaltered. *Ken Fairey/CA*

Northampton Bridge Street and beyond

This building, which stands to the south and west of Bridge Street station site, was, until 1881, the LNWR locomotive shed for Northampton. In 1882 a connection was laid between Bridge Street and Castle stations, and this shed went out of use in favour of a larger one with a better connection to the main line. The new shed could cater for 40 locomotives, and in 1959 had an allocation of 37. Though the antecedents of this smaller shed are still fairly obvious, by the date of this picture, 4 October 1994, the building was in use by the Civil Engineer's Department.

Still there on 24 August 1999, it is less obviously an engine shed, from the end at least, though the side of the building still gives an indication of its past. The area is still in use by Railtrack as a Civil Engineer's depot. *Ken Fairey/CA*

Northampton Bridge Street had one of the handsome Livock-designed Tudor-style buildings that several of the stations along the Nene Valley line enjoyed. The gables and chimneys are reminiscent of those at Wansford (which survive), but the building itself looks bigger – which is, of course, only right and proper for an important town such as Northampton. By the 1830s Northampton was England's premier boot and shoe centre, and a third of the population was involved in the trade. The train calling at the station is once again Ivatt 2-6-2T No 41225 with its 'Wellingborough Motor' on 2 May 1964. One can't help feeling that if this were running today there would be rather more people around to see it off than just our photographer.

Rails serving the Civil Engineer's depot are still there, and trains were in evidence on both occasions I was there, so the signal for the level crossing, though almost shrouded in foliage, sees reasonable use. I estimate that the building shown in the previous picture stands beyond the prominent bush in the centre. Note the former engine shed to the left, behind what would have been the western end of the up platform. *Ken Fairey/CA*

As road traffic built up on Bridge Street over the years one imagines that this level crossing must have become something of a bugbear. The wheel that was used to operate the gates is clearly evident in this picture, another from 2 May 1964, as the ubiquitous taper-boilered 2-6-2T No 41225 leaves Bridge Street station and crosses the road for one of its final trips along the line to Wellingborough. The carriages are LMS-design non-corridor suburban stock, and one wonders about the stock standing in the distance on the up line. Meantime, as the train passes, the signalman completes the train register, his 'black box' of events during his shift. The signal box itself is an LNWR Type 4 box, built in timber on a brick base that contains the locking-room.

Left It's nice to see a signal box still in working nick! Something is expected, but not for the moment, so the signaller has a chance to watch the passing road traffic instead. The second line of rails has gone, and barriers have replaced the traditional gates, so no doubt the gate wheel in the box has gone too. But the box looks pretty much as it did in 1964, even to the BR-style nameboard. The left-hand bargeboard has been renewed, and is now a better match for the right-hand one, which remains unchanged – or is that mere coincidence? But the characteristic two-ended finial and ventilation slot are just as they were. *Ken Fairey/CA*

Below Sketch map of the lines around Northampton Bridge Street station.

The legend along the front of the crossing cabin is indistinct, but appears to read 'Little Houghton Crossing'. There was no station at Little Houghton, but the line crossed a minor road on the level about a quarter of a mile to the south of the river. A train hauled by a Midland Railway tank locomotive is approaching from the Wellingborough direction while both the crossing-keeper and his wife (perhaps) keep a sharp eye in the photographer. Note the exceptionally tall LNWR-type signals – presumably high for sighting purposes, though there seems to be nothing in the vicinity that might obscure them.

All trace of railway has gone by 24 August 1999, and the only indication is a change of fencing on one side of the road and a gateway on the other. The signal box and the attractive crossing-keeper's cottage have vanished, but is it possible that the shrub immediately behind the signal post in the 'past' view is the substantial tree to the right of the gate in the 'present' one? *Deacon, NVR Archives/CA*

A better view of the crossing-keeper's cottage at Little Houghton, taken, it is thought, during the 1890s. It stood on the north side of the line, in the eastern angle between the road and the railway, the signal cabin placed on the other side of both. The two-family picnic party has dressed in its best finery for the outing, it seems, though all appear slightly apprehensive, perhaps at the thought of what the photographer may do to their features! Whether it is the finery or the photographer that is causing the comment among the folks near the level crossing gate is anyone's guess.

The road looks more substantial on 24 August 1999, but cottage, signal cabin and picnickers are no more, and the field they enjoyed is solidly fenced off. Instead of an ancient perambulator, today's photographer has managed to include the front of his own 'chariot'. *Deacon, NVR Archives/CA*

An eastbound train halts at Billing station, again probably during the 1890s. Billing Road (it retained the 'Road' suffix only until 1 April 1883) first appeared in the timetable in December 1845, so was almost certainly not one of the 'partly built stations' that the Directors had seen during their journey along the line the previous summer. Having come in late, it also failed to see out the full life of the line, at least so far as passengers were concerned, for it closed in 1952. Goods traffic did hang on until the end, though. The train is hauled by an '18-inch Goods' locomotive (18 inches being the length of the cylinder stroke) with 5-foot diameter driving wheels, one of a type that carried the LNWR crest on its central wheel-splasher. Their official alternative designation was 'Crested Goods', but they became more popularly known as 'Cauliflowers' from the shape of the crest. The stock is a rake of six-wheelers dating from before 1874, when the LNWR began to build bogie stock, headed by a four-wheeled carriage.

Had the station managed to survive until the 1970s it might have done some good business, for a few hundred yards away there is now Billing Aquadrome, which attracts many thousands of visitors each year. No trace of the station itself remains on 24 August 1999, however, though the main house in the group shown here is, in fact, the one-time station house. *Deacon, NVR Archives/CA*

One of Stanier's '6P/5F' 2-6-0 engines, No 42982, passes the closed Billing station en route for Northampton on a damp 24 April 1964. This engine was the last but two of a group of 40 built to a Stanier taper-boiler design introduced in 1933. With a '5MT' classification, they weighed only 69 tons 2 cwt, and worked to a boiler pressure of 225psi. One of the class survives – as No 2968 – on the Severn Valley Railway. Here at Billing, the small goods yard, comprising a loop and a siding, lie behind the train as it heads west; these facilities closed on 1 June 1964.

All the nearest buildings of this group, photographed on 24 August 1999, are post-railway, but the distinctive hipped roof of the house behind marks it as the same as that shown in the previous 'past' picture. The passing white van marks the site of the level crossing, and the buildings beyond the road cover the site of the goods yard. No sign of the railway is now visible from the road. *Ken Fairey/CA*

The next station was Castle Ashby & Earls Barton. Earls Barton takes its name from a barley farm that belonged to the Earl of Huntingdon, and Castle Ashby is the country seat of the Marquis of Northampton. When the station was opened, however, only Castle Ashby was used for the name, to which '(White Mills)' was added for some corn mills near the river only a few yards from the railway. In May 1869 the suffix was replaced by '& Earls Barton', the name that lasted until the end. The only buildings here were those of the station and a signal box – just to be seen through the smoke of the passing train on 30 April 1964, with our old friend No 41225 heading towards Wellingborough with the 'Motor', though not, this time, on the final day of service.

Who would guess that a railway ran here once? The railings represent what were once level crossing gates, and the buildings of the previous picture rested in the shrubs on the right. The signal box stood behind the low wall, where the conifers now are, but at least the road is still in the same place! In fact, a railway presence has been retained, because the goods yard (beyond the conifers to the left) is now the site of a restaurant, using railway carriages as part of its accommodation. *Ken Fairey/CA*

Wellingborough

Opposite The population of Wellingborough was 5,000 when the railway arrived – and as at Peterborough, the London & Birmingham, later the LNWR, was first in the field. It was also the third largest shoe-making community in the county, but the station was built (no doubt for geographical and topographic convenience as much as for anything else) at a level crossing on the turnpike road to the south. It was a site that, as road traffic grew, became an increasing source of embarrassment to the railway. Some trains stood at the platform foul of the crossing, and shunting movements often made matters worse. In August 1961 Fairburn 2-6-4T No 42104 approaches the infamous crossing with a Peterborough-bound train. These locomotives were a 1945 development of the earlier (1935) Stanier two-cylinder taper-boiler design. The wheelbase was made shorter on the Fairburn version, but aside from this the alterations were in matters of detail. They weighed 2 tons 12 cwt less than the Stanier version, generating the same tractive effort of 24,670lb.

The nearest equivalent to the footbridge vantage point these days is the flyover carrying the dualled east-west A45 road across the site of the level crossing. The angle is slightly different, but this is what one could see almost exactly 38 years later, on 16 August 1999. The railway's trackbed ran through the low brick wall, along the access road between the truck and girder pile and curved behind the prominent tree. The open area to the left of the site entrance was the location of the War Memorial and it may just be possible that the small section of fencing visible between the gatepost and the bush is the post-and-bar fencing shown in the original picture... *Ken Fairey/CA*

Above A view of the crossing from the rear window of a Northampton-bound train on 29 April 1954. Wellingborough London Road was another of the 'Tudor' station buildings, though the curved gables of Northampton are here made simpler and straight. The main building was on the down (Peterborough-bound) side, which was also the side on which the town lay, and where there was a substantial flour mill belonging to Messrs Whitworth. Rail access to this was beyond the platform, via a siding and wagon turntables. Beyond that again was Wellingborough Midland Junction, laid in by the Midland in 1866 as a link to its station on the north side of the river. The War Memorial was moved to a site on the opposite side of the road near the flyover embankment when the road system was modified. *H. C. Casserley*

Another view of the level crossing, but from the lineside to the left. On 1 May 1964 one of Stanier's Class '6P/5F' 'Moguls', No 42946, pauses at London Road – due away at 4.53pm – on its journey from Peterborough to Northampton. No 42946 was a Crewe North engine in 1959, so had made a journey south at some point. The footbridge, which lay on the station side of the level crossing but did not have access to the platforms, was invaluable to pedestrians at such times as those depicted here.

Left The site of the 'past' photograph now belongs to a firm of light engineers, Fredon Engineering Ltd. On 16 August 1999 the flyover, you might feel, makes a poor substitute for the footbridge, though road users are probably happier. The re-sited War Memorial can just be glimpsed to the right of the stack of steel girders, between the branches of the bush. *Ken Fairey/CA*

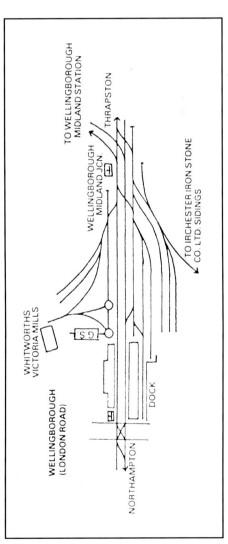

Left Sketch map of Wellingborough Midland Road station.

WELLINGBOROUGH
(LONDON ROAD)

NORTHAMPTON

DOCK

WHITWORTHS
VICTORIA MILLS

GS

WELLINGBOROUGH
MIDLAND JCN.

TO WELLINGBOROUGH
MIDLAND STATION

THRAPSTON

TO IRCHESTER IRON STONE
CO. LTD. SIDINGS

On 5 December 1960 '4F' 0-6-0 No 44340 heads a goods train across the level crossing towards the spur up to the Midland line and Wellingborough Midland station. The Ford Zodiac and Vespa motor scooter (there's nostalgia for you!) will soon be on their way.

Well, if nothing else at least the traffic situation on London Road is easier now. The A45 flyover crosses the point where the level crossing once was, though at a more acute angle – the railway passed through the car-park on the left. Probably the most awkward thing for road traffic these days is turning right on to the A509 from the yard on the left. *Ian L. Wright/CA*

On 18 April 1964 Brush Type 2 diesel No D5670 rumbles into Wellingborough London Road station with a Peterborough-bound train. The signal box is another LNWR Type 4; note the line of firebuckets hanging below the board instructing passengers that the bridge is the only way across the line, and that they can't get out that way.

Whitworth Bros now own the whole of the station area, part of which is leased out to other enterprises. By 16 August 1999 the site is given over to the parking for cars beside the embankment of the flyover. *Ken Fairey/CA*

Wellingborough London Road on 28 May 1960. Behind the up-side building the open wagons are standing beside a goods dock, stock pens of which can be seen. The ironstone sidings lay beyond. The up-side building itself consists of little more than waiting rooms, toilets and canopy. Beyond the train are the lines to the flour mill, Midland Junction signal box, and the line curving left to Midland Road. As for the train, Stanier Class '5MT' 4-6-0 No 45374 is heading the 4.54pm departure for Northampton, from Peterborough. It bears a 1A shedplate, so we have a visiting Willesden engine here.

The ironstone sidings area is now a helicopter pad, while to the left is the only thing which has been consistent throughout – the flour mill. I was told that some of the rails leading into it are still in place. Whitworth Bros has developed a good deal since 1960, and the facility now performs a much wider distribution function than it did then. The distant white-roofed building with the black-capped tower on the horizon lies nearly opposite the site of the junction with the Midland main line. *Ken Fairey/CA*

Looking from the up platform we see Fairburn 2-6-4T No 42062 running in with a train from Peterborough on 27 April 1964. The shedplate is not clear, but could be 1H, indicating Northampton – it had been renumbered from 2E in the previous year. Facilities on the up side at Wellingborough were not palatial, but at least passengers had a canopy to shield them from the weather, which is more than could be said for some smaller stations along the line. On the left the lines leading to the flour mill can be more clearly seen, and, beyond the signal box, the tracks leading up to Wellingborough Midland.

By 16 August 1999 the 'business' end of the old station was given over to parking for cars – and how many sharp-eyed readers can spot the helicopter beyond the mesh fencing? *Ken Fairey/CA*

We move to the north end of Wellingborough London Road's up platform for the next picture, taken on 25 April 1964. Brush Type 2 diesel No D5586 is approaching with a train from Peterborough, while the raised signal above the train indicates that Ivatt '2MT' 2-6-2T No 41227 is taking a 'Motor' up to Wellingborough Midland. Type 2 engines by Brush Traction of Loughborough were supplied between 1957 and 1962, and have proved to be one of the longest-lasting diesel types so far, some being still in service more than 40 years on. Several are also in preservation, so are likely to be around for a while yet. The actual junction of the line to the Midland station lay just beyond the signal box visible behind the oncoming train. The flour mill sidings trailed into the main line just on this side of the signal box, while the lines on the right led to the goods dock and to the Irchester Ironstone Company's sidings.

Today's view provides another of those pictures where perhaps the least said the better. All one can say with reasonable certainty is that the location is somewhere around where the up platform end once was, and that the gap between the bushes to the left of the gate may have been the site of Wellingborough Midland Junction. *Ken Fairey/CA*

A distant view of Wellingborough London Road from north of the river on 26 June 1957. The station buildings are on the extreme right of the picture as Beyer-Garratt 2-6-0+0-6-2 No 47969 blasts its way up towards the Midland main line with a rake of opens. The two original engines of this type were introduced in 1927, and the remainder of a class, numbering 33, had been built by 1930 for the London coal traffic along the Midland main line. They weighed 155 tons 10 cwt. Wellingborough had an important freight shed, with an allocation of 63 steam engines in 1959, housed in two enclosed roundhouses. One of these was demolished in 1964 to make way for a new diesel depot.

On 16 August 1999 the bridge abutment on the extreme left confirms that this is indeed the same spot – but it's very hard to imagine a Beyer-Garratt blasting through the undergrowth today. *Ken Fairey/CA*

'The Cobbler' – obviously chosen to reflect the predominant industry of the area – was the name of a railtour run on 19 September 1964, after regular passenger services had ceased on the Nene Valley line. It traversed the link line between the two Wellingborough stations, and here we see it as it crosses the river and approaches the Midland line junction. It is hauled by Class '4F' 0-6-0 No 44414, bulled up especially for the occasion. These engines were a post-Grouping development of a 1911 Midland design, introduced in 1924 in a series totalling 580 engines. They had 5ft 3in diameter driving wheels and worked at a boiler pressure of 175psi.

The fence beside the river path – or one very similar – was still there on 16 August 1999, and so was the brickwork of the arches, but vegetation has taken over, the rails are gone, and there would be very little chance of running an excursion here now... *Ken Fairey/CA*

Opposite From the end of the up platform at Wellingborough Midland Road, looking south, we see 'Patriot' Class 4-6-0 No 45541 *Duke of Sutherland* heading southwards through the back road on 27 May 1960; the shedplate (2A) shows it to have been a Rugby engine at the time. It is running with a Fowler tender to which additional coal-rails have been fitted. Wellingborough Junction signal box clearly does not date from Midland days – it is a replacement box dating from 1943. The link line down to Wellingborough London Road lay to the right of the small white building beyond the signal box.

Not a lot remains that is identifiable on 16 August 1999, though the Midland main line is still in place. The signal box, closed in 1983, has gone; the link to London Road diverged between the two colour-light signals. *Ken Fairey/CA*

Looking into the station we see Ivatt 2-6-2T No 41224 waiting to leave with the return 'Northampton Motor' on 21 June 1962. *Ken Fairey*

East through Thrapston

The first stop east of Wellingborough was Ditchford, an attractive little station on the north bank of the river. Alas, its attraction did not count for much, for it was the first station on the line to lose its passenger service as long ago as 1924. It was the first, also, to lose goods facilities, but that was at least delayed until 1950. There is, in fact, no village, and it is a little difficult to decide why a station should have been thought necessary, though the bridge and the three mills here had been an important site in medieval times. The platforms were short, and the 'facilities' were never more than a wooden building attached to a small station house. Our picture, taken on 18 May 1962, shows the Irthlingborough school train approaching Ditchford from the west behind Ivatt 2-6-2T No 41218.

On 16 August 1999 a hedge has replaced the fence, and the telegraph poles are different, but the view (taken from a little further back than the original) is very much the same – without, of course, the benefit of a train. *Ken Fairey/CA*

Irthlingborough lies some 2 miles along the valley from Ditchford, and boasted one of the Livock-designed large stations, like both the others we have seen so far, built in brick. Here, as at Wellingborough, there were straight gable-edges, but Irthlingborough had, for some reason, four gables to Wellingborough's three! The station was called Higham Ferrers at first, reflecting the importance of the boot and shoe town, but local representations in 1885 changed it to Higham Ferrers & Irthlingborough. In October 1910 it assumed its final name – Irthlingborough is, after all, very slightly nearer! Behind the locomotive in this picture is the goods shed, like all the others along the line placed at right angles to the railway. On 21 April 1956 an evening train from Peterborough to Northampton is headed by No 62568, a Class 'D16/3' 4-4-0 introduced in 1933. This particular version was a rebuild of an original Class 'D15' of 1904, with a large round-topped boiler and modified footplating.

We are well into the gravel extraction belt now, and the conveyer overhead is carrying the product across the road, whose level crossing survives, though the gates do not. The trackbed (and there was still at least one rail still in situ on 24 August 1999) forms access points to the gravel workings in both directions, and is private property. *Ian L. Wright/CA*

This overall view of Irthlingborough was taken in September 1963 from the concrete viaduct carrying the A6 over the river and railway, as an unidentified Class 'B1' 4-6-0 locomotive draws away westwards with a Northampton train. The picture emphasises the siting of the goods shed at right-angles to the main line of railway. In these circumstances, of course, access could not be made by engines, and wagons were manoeuvred in for loading or unloading by means of wagon turntables, though in this particular case direct rail access was later made through a side entrance. Some idea of the comparatively easy terrain that the line ran through can be gained from this picture.

The 'present' picture (taken on 26 May 1999) only emphasises how complete the destruction of the station has been – everything has gone, even down to the gateposts. Trees screen our view of the trackbed between the station site and the bridge, and also the only remaining feature – the level crossing. *Ian L. Wright/CA*

A fine shot of ex-Tilbury 2-6-4T No 42353 on a wintry morning in March 1958 as it calls at Irthlingborough with a Northampton to Peterborough train. These engines dated from 1927, Fowler's original parallel-boiler design for the LMS of a tank engine to work the passenger traffic on the Tilbury line out of Fenchurch Street. There was an imposing building on the main platform, but very little in the way of facilities on the up side. The entrance to the goods yard, which lay behind the main station building, was at the east end of the up platform. In the background can be seen the A6 viaduct, a notable feature of the local landscape.

On 26 May 1999 the concrete viaduct comes into its own as the only identifiable feature from the previous picture – it can just be seen crossing the trackbed, but is much more noticeable as it strides northwards towards the river. Beyond this watercourse can now be found the headquarters of one of the most improved non-league football clubs in recent years, Rushden & Diamonds. *Ian L. Wright/CA*

Another picture from the level crossing end, this time taken in September 1963, as Stanier Class '5MT' 4-6-0 No 45302 starts away from Irthlingborough with a Northampton-bound stopping train. This is a Northampton engine, the shedcode having become 1H in that year, the clarity of the plate perhaps reflecting this very thing. Sharp-eyed readers will by now, no doubt, have recognised the characteristic ventilation slot and double-ended LNWR finial on the gable of the signal box.

Now that station and train have both gone, the view along the trackbed on 26 May 1999 is clearer but perhaps less interesting. The conveyer continues for some miles. *Ian L. Wright/CA*

Ringstead & Addington was at first named only for Ringstead, the nearest village, but Addington was added in 1898. The station had staggered platforms, one on each side of a level crossing. Approaching from the west in early 1957 is a freight train bound for Thrapston Bridge Street. The locomotive's number is not noted, though its Class can be identified as a '4F' 0-6-0 of Midland parentage, but of a type introduced in 1924, so actually an LMS engine. Note the oil-lamp, still in use in 1957 and probably remaining unchanged to the end.

There is hard evidence in this picture of the farm usage to which the trackbed is currently put. Perhaps the main contrast between 1957 and 26 May 1999 is the increased amount of vegetation. *Ian L. Wright/CA*

Photographed on the same day as the previous 'past' shot (witness the bicycle) in early 1957, a Peterborough to Northampton train pulls away from Ringstead & Addington powered by Class '2P' 4-4-0 No 40683. The building on the left was the main station building here – and the bicycle looks about the smartest item on the platform! The siding in the foreground was put in for transhipment to standard gauge of the ironstone coming from the extensive narrow gauge system of Butlin's, who had mines between here and Ringstead village. This enterprise opened in 1871, and at first produced about 1,000 tons of ore a week, which was carried to the station in horse-drawn wagons until the internal railway was built, but it closed after about 20 years.

By 20 August 1999 the site had been completely cleared, and gave access to farm property behind the cameraman, whose car is parked on approximately the site of the hut on the right of the 'past' picture. *Ian L. Wright/CA*

The up side platform was the first reached by up trains, so that as Class '4F' 0-6-0 No 44522, heading for Northampton, passes on 23 May 1957 it obscures the platform from the camera. The station was in an isolated spot, at the end of a track from Ringstead village that ceased shortly after it crossed the line between the platforms, and passenger facilities provided were basic. There were, however, a number of ironstone quarries hereabouts, which made connections with the main line. Most were worked out by the beginning of the 20th century, but despite this the goods service at the station was maintained until March 1964.

By 20 August 1999 there was no sign of either platform, and the trackbed in the northerly direction was being walked. The road from Ringstead is probably more used now than it was, however, for it forms a section of the Nene Valley Way, a leisure walk. Apart from the low embankment, one point of reference remains – a post halfway down the slope on the far side of the lane, just to the left of the end of the nearest line of fencing. *Ian L. Wright/CA*

The London & Birmingham branch was the first railway into Thrapston, establishing itself at a site near Bridge Street some 20 years before the Midland sponsored a line from Kettering to Huntingdon, opened in 1866. It had to cross the river valley – and of course the railway along it – and did so originally by way of what has been described as a somewhat rickety viaduct. This picture shows the task of replacing the old viaduct with a substantial blue-brick structure in 1919/20, which was used until the line crossing it closed in 1959.

The new viaduct carrying the A14 trunk road dominates the valley today, and the old one can actually be seen better now from the new, which passes a few yards to the south of it. The old is not totally obliterated, however, and visible here on 19 May 1999 above the old arches is the spire of Islip church, a constant that one might expect to be around for a good few years yet. *Thrapston Historical Society/CA*

Thrapston station's layout was not dissimilar to that at Oundle, though Oundle's platforms were staggered, as we shall see. It had a Livock-designed station building, too, on the up side, which appears to be of stone – the chimneys and wing-walls certainly are, implying perhaps that the rest is too, though under a magnifying glass the main walls look as if they have been rendered, who knows when? A smaller gable in the centre is a variation – this appears on the other side at Oundle. The level crossing lies behind the photographer in this 1950s view, and it is nice to see a couple of cattle wagons on the left – they look to be of LMS vintage. A water tower stands beyond the timber down-side building, at the Peterborough end of the station.

Today no trace whatever of the station survives, although behind the photographer in this March 2000 view the heavily overgrown trackbed can be found heading westward. The site is now occupied by the joinery business of Scotts of Thrapston, and the LNWR timber waiting room has been replaced by samples of wooden stables and summerhouses displayed on the former station site. *Stations UK/Will Adams*

Thorpe had a small station building on its down platform, which was reached just beyond an acutely angled level crossing of the A605 road between Thrapston and Oundle. The signal box stood beside the crossing – behind the cameraman in this first picture – and the road can be seen on the left. Access to the small goods yard, which consisted of a loop, a spur and a siding, can be seen beyond the station platform. Six trains each way called here daily in the last year of operation, and local goods services lasted for two months after closure of the line, by means of an out and back service from Peterborough.

The building may be much changed but at least it has survived – this is how it looked on 4 October 1999. The square extension at this end has been heightened and gabled, and to its left can be seen the original gable line of the 1840s house. Both the lower-floor window spaces have been retained, as have the window and doorway of the extension to the left, while the access from the square room now leads into the conservatory. The chimney-stack style has also been maintained. Would that all conversions were so sympathetic. *Stations UK/CA*

Today the photographer would need to take his life in his hands to take this picture from the level crossing, showing the location of the signal box in relation to the station at Thorpe. The gate we can see would have had to make a very long swing in order to bar the road, such was the angle of the crossing. I have to say, however, that though in my youth I must have used this crossing a good many times I never remember being held up at it for a train.

The view from the same place on 19 May 1999 is not wildly inspiring, the owner of the station building, very sensibly in the author's view, wishing to cut off today's heavy traffic from the peace of his garden as much as possible. *H. C. Casserley/CA*

The line left the river for a while to cross a spur, but began to close on it again as it reached Barnwell. The station master's cottage just visible on the right of this 1950s picture is a part of the original station, the timber waiting room and canopy being added only in the 1870s and now preserved at Wansford by the Nene Valley Railway. There was a small goods yard, recently built over, behind the photographer. With nearby Barnwell Manor being the home of the Duke and Duchess of Gloucester, the station was more than once visited by royalty.

The station master's cottage survives as a residence on 19 May 1999, and part of the down platform is still there beneath the undergrowth, but the rest, together with the trackbed beyond the station, now lies beneath the **Oundle bypass.** *Stations UK/CA*

Oundle

This picture from the footplate of a train approaching Oundle was taken in the early 1960s. The train is about to cross the river for the second time within a mile (though the river has flowed for 2½ miles in the meantime) and the signal box, signals and chimneys of Oundle station can be seen in the distance.

A similar viewpoint in August 1999 had to be taken beside the Oundle bypass, where the road bridge crossing the river uses the same site as the railway bridge but at a slightly different angle – hence the curve of the road to the right while the station buildings can (just) be seen straight ahead, above the bridge's railings. *R. Stewart-Hindley, NVR Archives/CA*

Oundle is home to two of the three Livock buildings to have survived on the Nene Valley line – the station building itself and the adjacent Riverside Hotel, now awaiting restoration and not, sadly, looking its best. The station is the 'straight-gable' style that we have already met, but previous examples were built in brick. Here and at Wansford Livock built in the local stone, though it's anyone's guess whether this has anything to do with the fact that it is these three buildings that have survived. This print is undated, but the facade of the building shows that a number of repairs/changes – the lean-to on the extreme left – have been made since 1845.

It is still a handsome building on 4 October 1999, though the construction of a new housing estate on the site of the goods yard does not assist in seeing it from the same place as the earlier picture. *Tony Hayward/CA*

This is the business side of the station as it was in the years shortly before closure – to judge from the trace of weeds in the foreground, it would seem that by now this platform was the only one in use. How many passengers, on looking out of the carriage window as the train drew to a halt here, might have imagined that they had reached somewhere called Ketton Cement?

A slightly more distant view on 19 May 1999 reveals the building in something of its true glory. The mark where the canopy once rested is apparent, and for what it is worth this writer at least thinks the building looks better (as a building) without it. The range of unaltered ground floor windows, for instance, are an architectural notability in themselves. *Tony Hayward/CA*

The staggered platforms at Oundle can be clearly seen in this vintage picture as an LNWR train pulls into the down platform hauled by an unidentified Webb 2-4-2 tank engine, possibly one of the batch of 40 2-4-0 tanks engines converted to 2-4-2 in the late 1890s. The train consists of six-wheelers in the standard white and blackberry-black livery of the LNWR. The track to the left of the down platform is not shown on station diagrams, but the water tower beyond is clear. The tower/chimney beyond the trains is not explained, however – assistance from readers would be welcome.

A couple of steps to the right to avoid foliage shows the station as it is now, complete with the housing development that has encroached from the goods yard on which it began to the trackbed where the down platform was once situated. The canopy has gone from the station building itself, but otherwise it seems to have survived reasonably unscathed. *Tony Hayward collection/CA*

This splendid picture, taken, it is thought, in about 1914, shows an incredible number of visiting fisherman (not to mention their wives) carrying their equipment from the station towards the river, where they were no doubt about to take part in a fishing match. Their use of the trackbed as a means of egress suggests that they have arrived from the Northampton end of the line, the down platform being staggered beyond the up one. The town, built well above river-level, and the church, with its tall, distinctive spire, can be seen in the background; the tall chimney belonged to a brewery.

Levels suggest that the previous picture was taken from an upstairs window in the station building. From ground level on 4 October 1999 not so much is visible, though the church spire can still be found. *NVR Archives/CA*

Oundle signal box and the stone-built oil-store are seen as they were in the early 1960s – the picture was taken from the east side of the level crossing. Note the postbox in the massive gatepost to the right, and, above it, the board directing would-be passengers to the station. The poster extolling the pleasures of Herne Bay adds a nice period touch. The side gate at the crossing allowed pedestrian access across the road when the main gates were closed.

The heavy stone gatepost, distinctive by its summit decoration, was still there on 19 May 1999, but not a lot else. The drip moulding that sheltered the board is still there too, but both board and postbox are long gone. The site of the level crossing now gives road access to the station house. *Tony Hayward/CA*

Oundle signal box was in a style that has become familiar as we have travelled along the line. The picture also gives us another view of the oil-store from a different angle. The position of the sun seems to indicate that both this and the last picture were taken on the same occasion.

One or two things remain on 19 May 1999 to confirm the location; the short length of stone walling that protected the signal box from the road is still apparently unchanged, as is the iron fencing that borders the road on the left. Removal of the enormous hoarding to the left of the signal box is, perhaps, an improvement, because the station building is now more visible. The bus stop has been moved a few yards further back towards the town, on the other side of the river, and has been provided with a shelter, another improvement. *Tony Hayward/CA*

Another vintage picture of Oundle station around the turn of the 20th century, as an LNWR train hurries in hauled by a Webb 0-6-0 'Cauliflower'. Webb introduced the class in June 1880, and they were the first LNWR locomotives to carry Joy valve gear – 29 of the engines were still in service with BR in 1951. The carriages are bogies this time, and the passengers on the down platform suggest that a train is due in that direction also. Note the signals beyond the crossing, arms for both directions being on a single post. The wagon turntable in the foreground gave access for wagons from the siding on this side of the line to the goods shed and yard that lay off to the left. It also appears to have been the means of access to the right-hand siding as a species of stub-point.

The similarly located picture on 4 October 1999 has nothing of the bustle of a hundred years ago, rather the pleasant peace of an English garden. *Tony Hayward collection/CA*

There was no station at Elton until 18 months after the line had opened, so the station, when it came, was built by the LNWR rather than the London & Birmingham. No doubt it was hoped that the villagers of Fotheringhay, Warmington and Nassington would use it also, although it ran a mile or more from all of them, including Elton itself. It may perhaps be concluded that they did not in any great numbers, though at its busiest, during the 1880s, there were six stopping trains here each way per day. After 1900 usage and the service dwindled, and closure came in 1953. The station building, of a noticeably different style to other buildings along the line, still stood on 30 September 1967, at which time trains had ceased to run along any part of the line.

Vegetation makes impossible a view of Elton from the angle of the 'past' picture. On 26 August 1999 the platforms lay buried in undergrowth, and the only identifiable (and also visible) artefact was the level crossing gatepost, the right-hand one of the nearside pair shown in the 'past' picture. *J. P. Alsop, author's collection/CA*

Here is another indication of how easy was the country through which the Peterborough branch was built. However, the picture is slightly misleading, for the major obstacle on the line, the ridge through which Wansford tunnel was cut, lurks less than a mile away. The train from whose footplate this view was taken in the early 1960s is approaching Yarwell Junction, the point at which the link line between the LNWR's route from Rugby towards Stamford converged with the Nene Valley line, trailing in from the left.

The terrain hasn't changed much in the intervening years, and the trackbed on 21 August 1999 was still clear enough. The tall signal has gone, and no trace of it remains, while Yarwell Junction, today the western limit of the preserved Nene Valley Railway, lurks in the boscage ahead. *R. Stewart-Hindley, NVR Archives/CA*

Wansford

The 616 yards of Wansford Tunnel were not constructed without a certain amount of difficulty. The contractor was a Mr Jones, of Sheffield, who began work in January 1844 by removing 136,000 cubic yards of spoil from the tunnel approaches. Three shafts were sunk, water from springs in one of which almost trapped a group of men. There seems to be no specific record of when the tunnel was actually completed, though we know it was open to visitors by 25 April 1845, having cost £7,486 17s. Stone portals were placed at each end, that at the Yarwell Junction (or western) end being more elaborate. This picture, dated 24 January 1971, depicts the Wansford end of the tunnel at a time when the track was in use only by the Peterborough East Engineer's Department.

The only difference between this picture and the previous one is that the location is about 20 feet higher, having been taken – on 8 September 1999 – from the bridge which, since 1964, has carried the A1 trunk road across the railway. By now the line is in use through the tunnel by the preserved Nene Valley Railway, and it is their stock that we see parked on the left-hand track, the other now forming the main running line. The tunnel mouth is somewhat overgrown, but in 1990 the structure was Listed Grade II. *Butler, NVR Archives/CA*

Wansford's station building is perhaps the epitome of the designs made by J. W. Livock for the railway, and its mellow stonework looks glorious in sunlight. It was built by a Mr Thompson, of nearby Barnack, at an estimated cost of £5,606. The only other building with ornate gables such as this was the now demolished station (built in brick rather than stone) at Northampton Bridge Street. The picture is dated 10 September 1954, and 13 years later the Wansford station building, no longer thought useful in railway terms, was sold to haulage contractor. In 1973 it was, like the tunnel, Listed Grade II.

As a Listed Structure one would not expect to see many changes to the outside appearance of this splendid building. Courtesy of the current owner, this picture was taken on 8 September 1999. *Author's collection/CA*

This is a Northampton to Peterborough train with a slight difference, having on this occasion taken the branch north from Northampton Castle and travelled via Market Harborough on 6 June 1954. This was a scheduled service, not a re-routed Nene Valley line train, the three-coach set having left Northampton at 5.31pm behind '4P' 4-4-0 No 41162. This picture, taken from the old footbridge, shows an uncluttered view west towards the tunnel, in the days when the A1 still crossed the railway by the level crossing behind the camera.

The 'present' picture, taken on 26 August 1999, can certainly be said to show a contrast! It is taken from the present NVR footbridge as ex-Swedish State Railway No 1178 enters the station with a Peterborough-bound train from Yarwell Junction. To the left is the Nene Valley Railway's locomotive department, including the recently restored Bulleid 4-6-2 'Battle of Britain' Class No 34081 *92 Squadron*. *T. J. Edgington, NVR Archives/CA*

Nene Valley Railway stock was moved to Wansford from the British Sugar Corporation site in Peterborough, where it had hitherto been stored, in time for an opening to the public of the Wansford Steam Centre at Easter 1975. Our 'past' picture dates from that weekend, a very significant one in the Society's history. It shows the diminutive Hudswell Clarke 0-6-0 industrial saddle tank locomotive *Derek Crouch* working the single-coach shuttle service, in push/pull fashion, through the tunnel to Yarwell Junction and back. Hunslet 0-6-0ST *Jack's Green* stands by on the right.

Development at Wansford has been steady since those early days. Apart perhaps from the rails, the only point of reference between this photograph – taken on 20 August 1999 – and the previous one is the A1 bridge on the left. Extended platforms on both sides, a locomotive shed on the left, signalling, a restoration shed and stock (reading from left to right) from overseas, BR and the Great Northern Railway give a comprehensive summary of what the railway has to offer these days. *Allan Mott/CA*

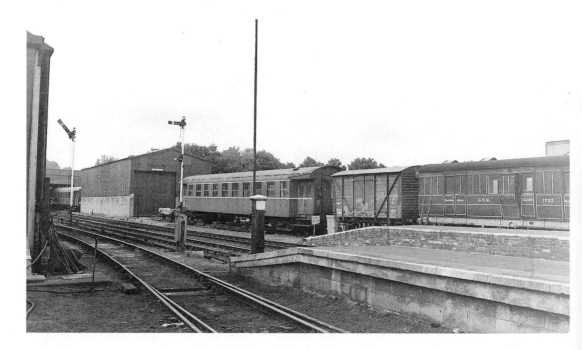

Another shot from the early days at Wansford, this time taken from the end of what was then Platform 1 in 1974, as BR Standard 4-6-0 No 73050 *City of Peterborough* approaches from the direction of the tunnel with a test coach. The A1 bridge is prominent behind the train, and the grounded railway van on the left looks as if it may be the sole storage space owned by the Society.

On 12 September 1999 the action is rather greater – on the left, with the roof of the locomotive shed above it and a water tower beyond, restored 'Battle of Britain' 'Pacific' No 34081 *92 Squadron* waits with a westbound train. Meanwhile ex-Swedish State Railway Class 'S' 2-6-2T No 1178 draws into the now renumbered Platform 2 en route to Peterborough from Yarwell Junction. These engines were widely used in Sweden on branch and suburban passenger trains, and 1178, after being placed in the Swedish military reserve in 1959, came to Britain in 1975. It was restored to steam the following year, and on 1 June 1977 worked on the NVR's inaugural train. Privately owned, it is now back in service after a full overhaul. *Allan Mott/CA*

This is the view eastwards from what was the end of Platform 2 on 31 March 1974. Until 1964 the level crossing took the railway across the A1, and was the cause of much frustration to road traffic. By the time the decision had been made to bridge the railway slightly to the west, rail traffic had already begun to fall off, and closure was only a matter of time – but it is interesting to speculate what the position of the railway society might have been when it was considering a site on which to begin its operations had the level crossing still been in use for heavy traffic.

These days, of course, the level crossing presents no problem, and is even the subject of some wonder as youngsters admire a type of crossing they may never have seen in action before. This picture, taken on 20 August 1999, shows a platform extended eastwards to the crossing, and the fine amenity centre opened by the NVR in 1995 as part of the celebrations marking the 150th anniversary of the railway's arrival in Peterborough. It contains offices, the railway shop, the buffet and toilets. The signals, genuine Great Northern somersault types, were rescued and restored from the closed branch between Holme and Ramsey. *J. H. Price, NVR Archives/CA*

Fowler 'Tilbury' 2-6-4T No 42350 stands at Wansford station on 25 August 1962, at the head of 'The Fernie' railtour train of the RCTS. There were 95 of these 1927 locomotives, and a 1933 variant introduced a side-window cab with doors, which must have made life a little more comfortable for the crews. In all there were five variations on this theme – the two Fowler versions mentioned, two by Stanier (in 1934 and 1935) and the fifth by Fairburn ten years later.

Platform 1 at Wansford is normally used for storing carriage stock these days, and 8 September 1999 was no exception. The buildings on the right remain substantially the same (though the fence has been renewed), but the view on the left has altered greatly. The canopy in the foreground is at the northern end of the new amenity building, while beyond is the NVR's main platform and building, with a footbridge across to Platform 1. The side of the locomotive shed can just be seen on the left beyond the footbridge, and the bridge carrying the A1, so prominent in the previous picture, is now very much in the background. *R. H. G. Simpson, NVR Archives/CA*

The final view shows Wansford signal box and level crossing on 24 January 1971. Services at the station had ceased seven years before, but a single track still ran through, and though the A1 bridge had also been built by now, the passage of any road traffic was not often inconvenienced by trains. In 1967 the down line beyond the station and through the tunnel became the Oundle line – for freight and to serve the school there – and the up line served the ironstone quarries at Nassington, just beyond the tunnel; they were worked on the one-engine-in-steam principle. The 60-lever signal box, an LNWR Type 5 with four bays to the locking-room and opened in 1907, closed in September 1971, and its rodding was disconnected. The reason for the sag in the fencing on the left is unexplained.

On 26 August 1999 the two tracks are back, the sag in the fence has gone, there is a splendid signal gantry and we can see the new amenity building from the eastern side. The level crossing gates remain unchanged, however, and the signal box...? Yes, the discerning will have noticed that it looks different, but it is, in fact, the same box beautifully restored with the correct LNWR configuration of glazing bars in the windows. Since 1990 it has been a Listed Structure under Schedule II. The river bridge was one of the 13 spanning the river along the line, and appeared in the LNWR register as No 56. *Butler, NVR Archives/CA*

Castor and Orton

This first view of Castor station, the next along the line, dates from around 1900 and is looking east towards Peterborough. The station lay about a mile from the village of Ailsworth – and even further from Castor itself, down a lane towards the river, which runs a quarter of a mile to the south. A stopping place was not opened here at once, and though a precise opening date is not known, the station was in the timetable by 1851. To judge by the extent of the buildings, however, great things were clearly expected, even at that distance from the community. Presumably some of the optimism was justified, for the passenger service survived until 1957 and the goods service for another seven years after that.

The second view is from a similar vantage point but later; although the print is undated, one suspects the late 1950s, perhaps shortly after closure, since the station sign visible beyond the building in the 1900 picture seems to have been removed. The two lamp-posts have also survived, one of them still with its top – and telegraph poles rarely changed in those days.

A V1 flying bomb landed near the station in January 1945 but was not responsible for removing all traces of the buildings from the scene; all it actually did was to rattle a few windows, dislodge a couple of slates and cut the telephone wires towards Peterborough. But this is the view from the same spot on 21 August 1999, and you need a fairly vivid imagination to conjure up a substantial small station. The aluminium tubular gates are definitely a come-down, and the telegraph poles, though still there, are in slightly different places. *NVR Archives/Rev R. Paten, NVR Archives/CA*

Looking westward back towards Wansford, this picture of Castor level crossing, though undated, was probably taken in 1971. Already a set of tubular gates has replaced the timber ones, and the old up line (on the left), despite the fact that it was by those days used as a siding and for training purposes, is well-maintained. A battery of signs on each side of the line warns anyone attempting to cross of the dangers inherent in arguing with a train.

The gate has been replaced again by 21 August 1999, and the bushes are bigger too, as ex-SSR No 1178 approaches the site of the station with the 11.20 from Wansford. It will call at Ferry Meadows – about 2¾ miles on – and Orton Mere, before reaching Peterborough Nene Valley at 11.45. *Butler, NVR Archives/CA*

A rake of three mineral wagons stands in the siding at Castor, perhaps awaiting collection after the ballasting session that appears to have taken place on the main line quite recently. Again the print is undated, but could well have been taken in 1971; the angle of the signal wire seems to indicate that the platform is no longer there, and gives another pointer for the date to be at least after 1965.

A similar vantage point on 21 August 1999 shows no wagons and a great deal of foliage. In the distance the Nene Valley Railway's 11.20 from Wansford can just be seen disappearing eastwards in the direction of Peterborough. *Butler, NVR Archives/CA*

This view eastwards from Castor Mill Road bridge was taken in 1948 – in the distance is the last of the 13 bridges across the river before the Nene Valley line reached Peterborough. Perhaps the feature that strikes us today about this picture is how well maintained the cuttings sides and trackbed of the public railway were, even fairly soon after a World War that had left everything in a very run-down state. Sleepers lie beside in the cess, waiting perhaps for a spot-resleepering session, and no train-timer would be likely to have difficulty in sighting the quarter-mile post.

From the same spot on 21 August 1999 the trackbed, now single, is still well-maintained. The sleepers have long since gone, but a quarter-mile post – of a different pattern and placed lower down the cutting side – is still clearly visible. The approaching train, hauled by ex-SSR No 1178, is the 12.00 service from Peterborough Nene Valley to Wansford, due to arrive there at 12.25. *Rev R. Paten, NVR Archives/CA*

A permanent way train is working 'wrong line' near Lynch river bridge in about 1950. The locomotive is in such a filthy state that the number is indecipherable even at these close quarters, but it can at least be recognised as a '4F' 0-6-0. There were a great many of these, introduced in 1924 as a development of a Midland design. A handful in the series had appeared two years earlier, built for the Somerset & Dorset Joint Railway – they were taken into LMS stock in 1930. A Royal Train was stabled in Lynch cutting for the night of 8 July 1971.

On 8 September 1999 foliage is once more rampant, and the rails on which the '4F' was running no longer exist. Nor does the bridge that crossed the line in front of the arched bridge, though traces of abutments can still be seen in the undergrowth. Perhaps in deference to the NVR's use of the Berne gauge, the track beneath the bridge has been slewed to the centre of the trackbed so that the stock can use the highest part of the arch. *Rev R. Paten, NVR Archives/CA*

This station, named Overton at opening, was renamed Orton Waterville on 1 August 1913, though it actually lay at that time in the parish of Orton Longueville. This was, allegedly, to avoid confusion with other Overtons, but did no one recall Water Orton, on the Midland line between Nuneaton and Birmingham? Like many places along the Nene Valley line, however, it was a substantial distance from its community, and this may have had a bearing on the fact that the passenger service, withdrawn perhaps as a wartime economy on 5 October 1942, was never resumed after hostilities had ceased. Goods traffic fared better, and continued until 28 December 1964. In the first picture, taken around 1900 and looking towards Northampton, two members of staff stand with two members of the public, presumably passengers. The signal box, of the type with which we have become familiar in these pages, looks new, and the rodding between the tracks leads to the pointwork for the small goods yard, behind the photographer.

By 6 July 1957 the platform shelter has gone, though the signal box can just be seen behind the engine in this indistinct but interesting view showing a Birmingham New Street-Clacton excursion passing Orton Waterville station hauled by Stanier Class '5' 4-6-0 No 44914. A long-armed lower-quadrant signal can just be seen above the roof of the station house on the left.

Today the platform, though a new one, lies in much the same place as it did in 1900, and the NVR's station building, recovered from Peterborough, looks a deal more substantial than the LNWR version. However, the signal box, demolished in 1968 after about 90 years' service, has gone, as have the platform and buildings on the up side. The old goods yard area is now used for permanent way stock and storage by the preserved railway, and the crossing, no longer gated, is controlled by flashing lights. The road is now much busier that it ever was in the old railway's heyday, for it is the main access to Ferry Meadows, the city of Peterborough's country park, and it is this name that the station has borne since 1978.

Orton probably doesn't consider it a major claim to fame, but it is of interest that C. J. Bowen-Cooke, who was the London & North Western Railway's Chief Mechanical Engineer between 1909 and 1920, grew up in Orton Longueville Vicarage. *NVR Archives/J. E. James, NVR Archives/CA*

Orton Mere lies only a mile east of Ferry Meadows, and was never a station on the old Nene Valley line. On 22 December 1982 the building work is under way in the shadow of Nene Valley Parkway, part of a system of dual carriageways that now encircles Peterborough.

By 8 September 1999 the building had been in use for 16 years, housing refreshment facilities for visitors and a ticket office, among other things. Perhaps the window, now bricked in, was originally intended to be part of this ticket facility. The Nene Valley Park is an area popular with cyclists, thoughtfully catered for by the cycle rack near the gate. *Peter Waszak, NVR Archives/CA*

From the railway side it all looks much more like a station as the builders keep at it on 22 December 1982, never mind that Christmas is only three days away! The raised signal seems a little optimistic, but the site had been in use as the eastern terminus of the NVR since 1 June 1977.

No one can have any doubt of the validity of the raised signal here. Orton Mere station carries a useful number of potential passengers as ex-SSR 2-6-2T No 1178 draws in on 21 August 1999 with the 15.37 arrival from Peterborough Nene Valley. With the opening of the extension to the NVR's Peterborough terminus (1986) a second platform was subsequently opened here on 23 March 1994, and can be seen on the left. *Peter Waszak, NVR Archives/CA*

This view is taken from St Botolph's bridge, which spans the looped link between the old Nene Valley line and the Great Northern Railway, usually known as the Fletton Loop. Here, just north of the bridge, was a wide array of sidings serving the premises of the British Sugar Corporation, and it is here on a summer's evening at some time before the Second World War that we see an LNER 0-6-0T arranging vans. Beyond the locomotive and signal box – a GNR specimen, though the details are indistinct – two long rakes of loaded open wagons await collection, while over on the right, in the distance, one of the BSC locomotives bustles about busily. You can almost hear the bees buzzing and smell the dog-roses…

Oh dear! Today the straight length of track in the foreground is the Nene Valley Railway's sole rail link with the outside world, but as for the rest perhaps it would be kinder to say nothing. In fact, this view has changed even since this picture was taken on 4 October 1999, for the area where the digger is being so busy is now taking shape as a housing estate. *NVR Archives/CA*

Peterborough Nene Valley and East

The LNWR built a locomotive shed at Peterborough, and though it had a trailing connection with the Midland before, together, they joined the Great Eastern at Peterborough East, it never directly linked with the Great Northern. The LNWR shed was over the photographer's right shoulder as he took this undated photograph looking west. The two tracks on the left were the running lines that went through to East. The river can just be made out between the raised calling-on signal and the telegraph pole to its left.

The two tracks through the platform at the NVR's Peterborough station more or less follow those of the LNWR, but there the resemblance ceases. The signal box is, of course, new and, in the name Woodstone Wharf, perpetuates the name of an LNWR box, though not on the same site. No longer can the river be seen, although it is only just beyond the trees on the right, and part of the trackbed, also on the right, is taken up with a cycleway/walkway that is part of the Nene Valley Park. The spur leading off the main line to the right is now access to storage sidings and the old shed compound, which houses Railworld. *NVR Archives/CA*

The LNWR shed faced west, and this aspect was therefore its entrance. In the early days of the line this site was used for coke ovens to fuel the locomotives, but in 1880 the LNWR built a five-road shed, with, off to the left and missing from this picture, a 45-foot turntable. There was also a large water tank, spanning two roads, and this can be seen to the left of the building. In 1932, with the LNWR and Midland both part of the LMS, the LNWR engines and crews were transferred to the larger (and more convenient) depot at Spital, opposite Peterborough North station. Long-ingrained company rivalries ensured that this move did not go as smoothly as it might have done! In this picture, taken in 1950, the shed looks remarkably respectable after 18 years of disuse. On the left is the Peterborough power station, with, in front of it, the bridge that crosses the river and carried the Midland line up to the level of North station. Behind the shed on the right is the south end of the girder bridge carrying the Great Northern Railway across the river and the Midland and Nene Valley lines.

Today the site of the shed is a compound that houses the Railworld collection of railway stock and artefacts from all over the world. It is open Monday to Friday in winter, daily in summer. Beyond is the East Coast Main Line girder bridge. *NVR Archives/CA*

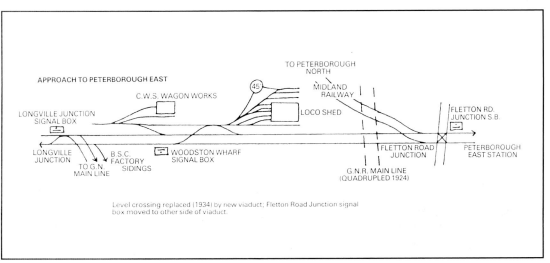

Sketch map of the approach to Peterborough East.

The shed's water tower survived in situ for some time after its use 'dried up', as it were. This picture was taken on 17 May 1964, by which time the two sidings beneath the tower had gone, but there was still a servicing road beside it. Beyond can be seen the Midland river bridge, the Great Northern river bridge, and the power station.

The point from which the last picture was taken is now inaccessible for photography, so this 8 September 1999 view was taken from somewhere near the far side of the former water tower. A two-car 'Sprinter' unit makes its way across the river round the curve towards Peterborough station and points west. On the right a board advertises Railworld. *Butler, NVR Archives/CA*

The present eastern terminus of the Nene Valley Railway is at a point just a few yards short of the old LNWR link with the Midland Railway before it reached Peterborough East station. This view, taken on 18 March 2000, is looking west towards Wansford. The sun is shining and the daffodils are out, but the coats of the passengers awaiting an imminent arrival from the west end of the line indicate a nip in the air. In the bay platform stands the railway's DMU. Note the cross on the signal arm at the end of the platform, indicating that it is out of use. The first train to this new station ran on 24 May 1986, and the extension was officially opened by HRH Prince Edward on **30 June.** *A. Mott collection*

Stanier '8F' 2-8-0 No 48726, of Aston shed (3D, closed in 1965), heads east with a freight train in about 1958, nearing the point at which the junction will be made with the Midland line, which can be seen curving away on the right. These engines, dating from 1935, weighed just over 72 tons (without tender) and quickly became such effective workhorses that they were among the last steam types to survive on BR through to 1968. A lucky configuration of the train allows us to see the LNWR engine shed in the background.

The same point today marks the eastern end of the Nene Valley Railway, the cars beyond the railings being parked with their bonnets towards a fence that screens the ex-Midland line. The roof of the Railworld exhibition – on the site of the LNWR shed – can be seen to the left of the bufferstops. *H. Cooke, NVR Archives/CA*

The Great Northern Railway's Nene Valley viaduct was built in 1849 by Thomas Brassey, and still incorporates today the oldest cast-iron bridge in the country carrying regular rail traffic. The original viaduct, carrying two tracks only, is the one on the far (east) side – that on the west was added in 1924, in what must have been an exercise not unlike that facing those who will shortly be building the second viaduct at Welwyn. This picture was taken in the late 1960s.

In the 'present' picture, taken on 8 September 1999, both the foreground and background have changed, but the railway interest is much the same. The power station is no more, and it has to be said that the car sales area in the foreground makes it look a lot tidier. Now also visible, in the foreground, is Peterborough's Oundle Road. *NVR Archives/CA*

Peterborough East was a station with character, and was built by the Eastern Counties Railway for the newly arrived line from Northampton, before they were themselves ready for it. It was simply Peterborough at first – until 1850 and the arrival of the Great Northern it had no competition. The station had a handsome building, whose facade appears to have survived pretty much in its original form throughout its life; this photograph, taken just before demolition, has striking similarities with an engraving published in the *Illustrated London News* at the time of its opening. The final Northampton train left at 8.49am on 2 May 1964, but the station did not close, for the line remained open for access to Nassington quarries and for coal trains to Oundle; there were also beginning/end of term specials for Oundle schoolboys. After June 1966 it was converted to a parcels sorting facility, in which function it continued until Christmas 1970. Everything except the platforms was demolished in April 1972.

On 26 August 1999 the far railings equate approximately to the south side of the old island platform, and it is a little difficult to imagine how two such substantial trees could have established themselves between 1972 and the present day. But all is not lost, for, despite appearances, there are still two tracks beyond the railings, as we shall see in a moment. *A. V. Fincham/CA*

At first Peterborough East had an overall roof, which appears to have been removed after an accident made it unsafe in 1887. Then in 1934 a road viaduct was opened to carry the busy London Road across the railway – it had previously crossed by an increasingly frustrating level crossing – and the East signal box was relocated on stilts at the west end of the platform, as can be seen here; beyond is the new viaduct. Though there was a footbridge, access to the island platform (on the left) could also be gained by means of a platform-level 'bridge', which station staff slotted into place as required. Something similar still survives in everyday use at Brockenhurst.

Commercial enterprises have taken over the station site at Peterborough East, and the area where the platforms once were serves as a car-park. The only point of reference left on 26 August 1999 is the road viaduct, now far and away busier than it was in 1934! *NVR Archives/CA*

Although this picture has the appearance of being older, it must have been taken after 1934 for it shows the view from the new road viaduct, looking east. After a few years as plain Peterborough this station became 'Peterborough (GE)' from the Great Northern's arrival in 1850 until 1 July 1923, when it took the suffix 'East', which it retained until final closure. The new signal box, set on legs across a single track, can be seen on the left. The short rake of horseboxes in the foreground, each with a groom's quarters, is of interest, and the signal is typical of those supplied to the Great Eastern by Mackenzie & Holland.

The 'present' photograph was taken a few yards to the left of the 'past' viewpoint, to avoid the trees. The fact that it is a Saturday explains the emptiness of the car-park, and from here a section of the old platform can be seen to the left of the approaching train. This is a Stansted-Liverpool service due off Peterborough North at 14.38, with unit No 158796 leading. In the centre distance, in front of the nearest of the pylons, is the Great Eastern engine shed, closed in the 1950s and used as a goods shed until 1970. Since then it has been in commercial use until recently, and was listed as a Grade II structure in 1992. *Mackenzie, NVR Archives/CA*

Peterborough North

This is the frontage of Peterborough North during the summer of 1958. An aura of mailbags seemed to hang permanently over the station, which above all is what this writer will remember Peterborough North station for. Goods facilities were all at this end of the complex, and the gabled building at the other end housed station offices. The hip-roofed tower is at the eastern end of the footbridge, whose span can be seen leading left. Taxis always seemed in short supply in those days, and would have made their exit past the photographer.

By 26 August 1999 it all looks very different. In the mid-1970s the station fabric was deteriorating, and it was decided that a rebuilding/remodelling operation should take place. The new station was opened by Sir Peter Parker on 30 September 1980, and has a much more clinical look – though it must be admitted that the smell of mailbags has vanished. There are many more taxis these days, too, which now all face the other way having an exit at the far end of the site. *H. P. White/CA*

This panorama of Peterborough North, seen from Crescent Bridge, to the south of the station, dates from 2 May 1959. The road that crosses the railway at this point had the same problem as that which crossed the river and the Nene Valley line to the south of the city – a level crossing that became increasingly congested. This one was solved earlier, however, for the bowstring girder bridge now known as Crescent Bridge was opened in 1913. In this picture a tank engine fusses with a van in the parcels bay (Platform 1), and what looks like an early diesel multiple unit is running into Platform 6, no doubt off the Leicester line. On the extreme left a southbound freight runs through on the up by-pass line.

By 8 September 1999 there has been a transformation in which there are three principal constants. One is the Great Northern Hotel on the right, the second is the southern end of Platform 3, and the third is a little more obscure, but is the factory in the distance on the left. The distant bridge is still there, though now obscured by the new footbridge. In the present layout the roads are, from left to right: Platform 5, used by trains using the cross-country routes between East Anglia and the Midlands; Platform 4, used also by cross-country trains, as well as down main line stoppers; next come the down and up through roads; then Platform 3, catering for the electric stopping services to London and DMUs on the Spalding and Lincoln route; and finally Platform 2, for the up main-line services, though since all the platform roads are signalled for bi-directional running, this occasionally also sees down trains. The train drawing in is the 14.32 departure; having started its journey at Leeds, with DVT No 82228 leading Class 91 No 91019, it will stop only once more, at Stevenage, before reaching King's Cross. The parcels bay on the right is Platform 1, lengthened and with a platform on both sides. The square-looking building above the incoming train is a mail-sorting centre. *A. E. Bennett/CA*

At the north end of the station Class 'A1' 'Pacific' No 60131 *Osprey*, with steam to spare, waits to enter Platform 2 with a Leeds-King's Cross express on 18 April 1960. The engine was only about ten years old at the time, and did not live out its normal life expectancy. The current A1 Project, under which a brand-new member of the class is being built at Darlington, should fill an important gap in our knowledge of locomotive history. The train itself looks an interesting mixture of carriage types and liveries. On the left a stopping train is about to leave for stations along the Midland line to Stamford, Oakham, Melton Mowbray and Leicester.

Well, yes, it is the same spot, though there isn't a great deal to prove it. The buildings in the background on the right are recognisable as basically the same, but that's about all. The goods dock and sidings in front of them have gone and the track alignments are much simpler, though the turnout to reach the platform from the bridge actually looks more awkward. The 'spaghetti' overhead gives a different feel as, on 26 August 1999, DVT No 82208 leads an up service for King's Cross only into the station. *Both CA*

Under the overall roof at Peterborough North on 18 April 1960, LNER Class 'A3' 'Pacific' No 60044 *Melton* draws in with a Leeds to King's Cross semi-fast. It could be gloomy under the canopy, even on a bright sunny day such as this, although the passengers' clothes seem to indicate that the April day is chilly in spite of the sun. Mind you, the least bit of wind under that canopy turned it into a sort of minor wind-tunnel. The 'A3s', designed by Gresley for the Great Northern Railway and introduced in 1922 as 'A1s', were developed over the years into a stable of 78 highly efficient machines, one of which, No 2750 *Papyrus*, held for a short time the steam speed record of 108mph, achieved in March 1935. Only one of the Class survives, the second built, now named *Flying Scotsman*.

Now it is 26 August 1999, the roof has gone and topcoats aren't necessary for once! The precise alignment of the platforms has shifted slightly, but this is near enough the same spot as HST power car No 43107 enters the station at the head of the 14.57 up 'Highland Chieftain' departure for King's Cross. All up trains on this afternoon were running slightly late following a power failure further north. *Both CA*

Back in the overall-roof days of circa 1880, Stirling 'Single' No 98 passes light engine through Platform 2 at Peterborough North. It would no doubt be heading for a headshunt at the south end of the station in readiness to take over a London express in due course. The Great Northern six-wheelers parked in the siding to the left of the engine would have been the crack vehicles of their day.

As we have already seen, the station looks very different now, although there was no problem in identifying the location for the equivalent shot. The sun disappears briefly on 26 August 1999 as DVT No 82228 is pushed by Class 91 No 91019 alongside Platform 2 at the head of the 14.32 for Stevenage and King's Cross. Though Platform 3 these days ends in more or less the same place as it did in 1880, the sidings at its southern end are long gone and the trackwork has been substantially remodelled, as we have already seen. *CA collection/CA*

INDEX OF LOCATIONS

'Companion' Volumes!